Equality

Equality
What It Means
and
Why It Matters

Thomas Piketty
Michael J. Sandel

polity

First published in 2025 by Polity Press

Polity Press
65 Bridge Street
Cambridge CB2 1UR, UK

Polity Press
111 River Street
Hoboken, NJ 07030, USA

ISBN-13: 978-1-5095-6550-4

A catalogue record for this book is available from the British Library.

Library of Congress Control Number: 2024945532

Typeset in 12.5 on 15pt Adobe Garamond
by Cheshire Typesetting Ltd, Cuddington, Cheshire
Printed and bound in Great Britain by CPI Group (UK) Ltd, Croydon

The publisher has used its best endeavors to ensure that the URLs for external websites referred to in this book are correct and active at the time of going to press. However, the publisher has no responsibility for the websites and can make no guarantee that a site will remain live or that the content is or will remain appropriate.

Every effort has been made to trace all copyright holders, but if any have been overlooked the publisher will be pleased to include any necessary credits in any subsequent reprint or edition.

For further information on Polity, visit our website:
politybooks.com

Contents

Note on the text

This book is an edited version of a conversation between Thomas Piketty and Michael Sandel, held at the Paris School of Economics on May 20, 2024.

1 Why worry about inequality?

Sandel:

Thomas, thank you for hosting us at the Paris School of Economics for this conversation about equality. One way of exploring what equality means is to begin by asking why inequality matters. Now, your research has revealed vividly to all of us just how stark are the inequalities of income and wealth. Let's begin with these inequalities. You've shown that in Europe the richest 10% take in more than a third of the income and own more than half of the property. And in the United States, inequalities are even starker. Many of us find this troubling, but why exactly is it a problem?

Piketty:

I'm very glad that we have the opportunity for this discussion.

Let me first stress that I am optimistic about equality and inequality. I make this point in my latest book, *A Brief History of Equality*, where I stress that, even though there's a lot of inequality today in Europe, in the US, in India, in Brazil – all over the world – in the long run there's been a movement toward more equality. Where does this movement come from? And this will be a way to answer your question. This movement comes from social mobilization and a strong, enormous political demand for equality of rights in access to what people perceive to be fundamental goods, including education, health, the right to vote, and more generally to participate as fully as possible in various forms of social, cultural, economic, civic, and political life. In your own work you've stressed the role of self-government and participation. And I think this appetite for democratic participation and self-government is also what has been driving this movement toward more equality in the long run.

Now, it's not been there forever, certainly not since prehistoric times. It starts in particular at the end of the eighteenth century with the French Revolution, the abolition of the privileges of the aristocracy, and with the American Revolution

to some extent. And it continues in the nineteenth century with the abolition of slavery, the
rise of labor movements, universal male suffrage,
and then the rise of universal female suffrage.
It continues in the twentieth century with the
development of social security, progressive taxation, and decolonization, and it has continued
even in recent decades. Sometimes we talk about
the neoliberal era starting in the 1980s as an era
of rising inequality. And it is true to some extent.
But in some dimensions of inequality, including
gender inequality, racial inequality, and North–
South inequality to some extent, the long-run
movement toward more equality has continued. And it's going to continue in the future, in
my view. Why? Because together with the rise
of modernity, you have the rise of democratic
awareness, an appetite for equal access to fundamental goods, to participation in all forms, to
dignity in all forms. And this is really the driving
force, including for the monetary dimensions of
inequality.

To conclude with your specific question about
income and wealth inequality, the numbers you
mentioned about today's high inequality levels
are correct, but they were even worse 100 years

ago. They were even worse 200 years ago. So there's been progress in the long run. It's never been easy. It has always involved enormous political battles and social mobilization. And it will continue like this. The good news is these are battles that can be won, and they have been won in the past. Studying these battles maybe is one of the best ways we have to prepare ourselves for the next steps.

Sandel:
You've just identified three reasons why inequality is a problem, as I hear you. One is about access to basic goods for everyone. The second is about political equality – voice, power, participation – and then you mentioned briefly a third: dignity. I'd like to see if we can isolate these three reasons why equality and inequality matter.

Let's suppose, hypothetically, that we had the same inequalities of income and wealth we have today, but that we could somehow insulate the political process from those economic inequalities. So, let's imagine that we could have public financing of campaigns with no private campaign contributions. Suppose we could regulate lobbying so that powerful companies and rich individuals could not have a disproportionate say in politics. Suppose we could somehow insulate political voice and participation from the effects of inequalities of income and wealth. And suppose we could address access to basic human goods – health, education, housing, food, transportation – through a more generous welfare state. So, we're imagining we could address the first concern, access to basic goods, and the second concern, access to participation and political voice, but still leave intact inequalities of income and wealth. Would there still be a problem?

Piketty:
I think there would still be a problem, in particular for basic dignity and in the human relations and power relations that come with inequality. Monetary distance is more than just monetary distance. It comes with social distance. Of course, companies' influence on politics and media is one of the most visible impacts of money on the public sphere. And it's very hard to imagine how we could solve this problem with the kind of income and wealth scale that you have today. But even if we could, taking your thought experiment seriously, you would still have enormous

inequality in purchasing power over the time of others. So, if by spending the equivalent of one hour of my income, I can buy your entire year of work, that implies kinds of social distance in human relations that raise very serious concerns and questions. So, the very formation of our ideals about democracy and self-government, which involves not only the formal organization of political campaigns and formal access to news, but also all these more informal relationships in our local community – social relations where people interact with each other, enter into deliberation with each other – is threatened by enormous monetary inequalities.

Finally, in my view, the most important political and philosophical argument is really a historical argument, which is that historically we've been able to address all of these concerns together. We've been able to reduce inequality enormously – not just access to basic goods and participation, but also monetary inequality in income and wealth. If you look at today, even with the rise of inequality in recent decades, the income gap in Europe between the top 10% or the top 1% and the bottom 50% or bottom 10% is enormously smaller than 100 years ago. This is less true in the US, but even in the US it is true as compared to 100 years ago.

So, we've moved toward more equality in the long run, and not only has this not been at the expense of prosperity or any other legitimate goals that we might want to balance with equality, but in fact this has been a key component of the rise of modern prosperity. Why? Because behind the enormous increase in prosperity that we've seen historically, the rise in a more inclusive and egalitarian socioeconomic system – in particular with more inclusive access to education – has been absolutely critical.

Now, there are two limits to that. One is that when we talk about access to basic goods, we have to keep in mind that the goods that we viewed as basic 100 years ago are not the same as today. So today a big issue is how you have a fair system of education, including at the level of higher education, an issue on which you have been writing and that we will talk about later. To keep it short for now, I think the fact that we've sort of given up on an ambitious egalitarian objective for higher education is at the source of many of our problems today – economic, and even more so democratic.

A second important caveat, which I want to stress right away, is the international and North–South dimension. So, a big part of the prosperity that we have in the North today, in Europe and in the US historically, has not only come through the rise of education and more inclusive investment in health and skills, which in a way is very positive – a win–win institutional transformation – but has also been made possible by the world division of labor. That's in effect the exploitation of resources – natural resources and also human resources – sometimes in a very brutal manner, and also with the extra cost, of course, of threatening planetary sustainability, which we see more and more today. And this to me is clearly the main limitation of this positive movement toward more equality and more prosperity that I was referring to as the main challenge for the future. But it is also one of the reasons why, in the end, I still want to be optimistic, because I think the only way to address these new planetary challenges is to go even further in the direction of equality than we imagined in the past.

2 Should money matter less?

Sandel:
Good. So, we've identified and already begun to discuss three aspects of equality: One is economic, a second is political, and a third is about social relations – about dignity, status, and respect. I'd like to come back to that third one shortly because it is in some ways the most challenging and maybe also the most intriguing. But I would like to go first to your proposals to deal with these three dimensions of inequality. The proposals begin with more progressive taxation, a fuller development of the welfare state, and inheritance taxes that can guarantee inheritance for all.

I'm sympathetic to all of these proposals. Some might say they amount to the kind of social democratic project that we already have, only a more robust version of it, aiming to realize it more fully. But then, reading your work, I notice a couple of potentially more radical proposals that might amount to a redefinition of the social democratic project beyond these more familiar proposals. One of them has to do with the transnational aspect, which is very interesting. But before we get to that, you write about a gradual decommodification of the economy and social life. And I'd like to ask you a question about decommodification in relation to redistribution, because the standard social democratic project is mainly about redistribution of income and wealth and therefore of political voice.

May I put to you another thought experiment, this one about redistribution and decommodification? Imagine two ways of dealing with the inequalities we've been discussing. One would be to try to redistribute income and wealth to give everyone more comparable purchasing power, but to leave the economy as commodified as it currently is. That's solution number one. Solution number two: to leave the distribution of income and wealth as it currently is, but to decommodify the economy and social life so that money matters less. So, for example, assume that the fundamental human goods could be decommodified – access to education, to healthcare, to housing, to political voice and influence and participation. Suppose we could decommodify social life to such an extent that the only real advantage of being wealthy would be the ability to buy things like yachts and caviar and cosmetic surgery or other luxuries. If we could choose one

SHOULD MONEY MATTER LESS?

of those two projects, radical redistribution while leaving commodification in place, or leaving the current distribution in place, but with a decommodification of social life, which would you go for?

Piketty:
First, on the way to answering the question, let me say that social democracy was once a radical project. So, when the Swedish Social Democrats come to power first in the 1930s and then after World War II, and when the Labour Party comes to power in 1945, they bring to power, including as ministers, people who left school at age 11 or 12 or 13. They bring people who were coal workers. They arrive in countries which had an aristocratic tradition – not only Britain, but also Sweden. Until World War I, Sweden was a country where only the top 20% of the male population could vote, and within this top 20% you had between 1 and 100 votes, depending on your wealth. And in municipal elections there was no ceiling, so that you had several dozen municipalities where only one individual had more than 50% of the vote and was a perfectly legal dictator. This was Sweden until World War I. This is where we

come from and I think it's important to realize that we've come a long way. This also shows that nothing is frozen, that the level of equality or inequality is not determined by permanent cultural or civilizational attributes, and that things can change through political mobilization.

I'll just pursue this example, because this will also bring me to decommodification: When the Social Democrats through the labor union movement took power in Sweden in the 1930s and 1940s, what they were able to prove, in effect, was that the state in itself is not pro-inequality or pro-equality. It depends on who controls the state and what you do with it. They were able to put the state capacity of Sweden to the service of a completely different project, where, instead of distributing voting rights depending on people's income and wealth, you make people pay a high progressive tax as a function of their income and wealth. And then you fund a system, including an education system, outside monetary logic and the profit logic.

This is what decommodification is all about and has been about historically. You take entire economic sectors out of the power of the profit motive. And the good news is not only that it worked, but that today these are very large economic sectors. Education plus health make almost 25% of the economy, much bigger than all manufacturing sectors together in developed countries. And they operate largely outside the profit logic, outside the shareholder-ownership model. And it works very well. In a country like the US where the health sector operates much more under the profit logic, you spend almost 20% of GDP on health alone, but with terrible outcomes as compared to European countries where systems are under the public logic. So, this decommodification worked historically. It was intimately related to redistribution and to the compression of the income and salary scale, and it happened through social democratic mobilization and trade union mobilization that were quite radical at the time.

Remember Hayek when he was writing about the "road to serfdom." He told his British and Swedish friends voting for Labour or the Social Democrats: "You are going to end up like the Soviet Union. You are going to end up with a dictatorship." Coming from someone who then supported Pinochet in the 1970s, being so afraid of the Swedish Social Democrats and the British Labour Party can seem funny today. But at the time these political movements were viewed as if the barbarians were going to take control of the state. In the end, they did quite well.

Now the problem is that social democracy, starting in the 1980s, and especially from 1990 or 2000 onward, after the fall of the Soviet Union, started to consider itself – or at least some of the leaders of social democratic parties did – as a sort of finished or frozen product. And this is a mistake, because the kind of transformation I imagine for the twenty-first century is of the same order of magnitude as the one which happened over the past 100 years. In my work I talk about participatory socialism and democratic socialism, a system which is quite different from the economic system we have today. But I would say it's not more different from the kind of social democratic society we have today than today's social democratic society is different from the capitalism of 100 years ago. The change would be of similar magnitude.

So, to the issue of decommodification, and I'm going to try to answer your question directly. Which one is most important? Is it the monetary compression of inequality or decommodification? If decommodification goes sufficiently far, it is clear that monetary inequality becomes almost irrelevant. So let's assume the economy is 99% decommodified. This will mean that 99% of goods and services, like education and health, are freely accessible. You only have 1% left commodified, and the monetary income corresponds to 1% of national income because, of course, national income should include – and does include to some extent in our accounting – public services that are available for free. So, if the monetary component of income is only 1% of national income, whether you have an income gap of 1 to 5 or 1 to 10 or 1 to 20 in this 1%, income is not very relevant. There will be actually no room for your expensive cosmetic surgery in this 1% because there will be very little purchasing power left. Now again, that being said, we should do the two at the same time because this is what has been done historically, and because the commodified share will be much larger than 1% for a long time ahead.

Let me stress this – that is, the historical rise of the social state. Some people prefer to say "welfare state." I prefer the notion of "social state" because it includes education, other public services, public infrastructure, and not just social security, strictly speaking. The rise of the social state historically has been made possible through the rise of labor unions, social security funds, social contributions to pay for these funds, but also through the rise of very progressive taxation and an enormous compression of the salary gap, the income gap, the wealth gap. We all know the basic story, but sometimes people forget how many countries saw the rise of the social state – not only Sweden, Germany, France, Britain, but also the US, which during many decades of the twentieth century had a top income tax rate up to 80%, 90%. From 1930 to 1980, the top income tax rate was 82% on average. Apparently, this did not destroy US capitalism. And, if anything, this was the time where the productivity of the US economy in terms of national income per labor hours was the highest in the world, with the largest gap with respect to other countries.

Why was this so? Because there was more widespread education in the US at the time, which was also visible to some extent in the twentieth century. In the middle of the twentieth century, the educational gap between the US and other countries was enormous. In the 1950s, 90% of the younger generation in the US went to high school. In Germany, France, and Japan at the time, it was 20% or 30%, and you had to wait until the 1980s to get to this almost universal access to high school. And this is the key to prosperity. In the middle of the twentieth century, the fact that you also had this 80% or 90% income tax rate on very top incomes and very top inherited wealth did not in the end have negative consequences for anything important. This compression of the income, wealth, and salary gaps was brought about not only by progressive taxation but also by minimum wages, and by an increased role for labor-union workers' representatives, which I would like to be a lot more powerful in the future on the boards of companies.

All that was very important. It's also what contributed to building a new social contract where the middle class would accept contributing to the social state. They knew that they would benefit from it, but also that people at the very top were going to pay a lot more than they would. Whereas today, of course, there's a big suspicion by the middle class – more than a suspicion – that people at the top are not paying their fair share. It makes them say, "Okay, then I'm not going to pay for people who are poorer than me."

So, the entire social contract that was set up in the twentieth century begins to unravel.

This progressive taxation was crucial, finally, because it is also what made it possible to regulate the economic power that arises when you have an enormous salary gap or income gap between the most well-paid people in the private sector and those in government. We were talking earlier about the effect of the monetary gap on dignity and social regulation, but it's also a question of efficiency. If you want to have the right people in your public-regulation agencies and they're paid 20 times less than people in Google, or wherever, you have a problem. And the solution is not to pay them 20 times more. The solution is obviously to reduce the salary gap enormously to compress the income gap. Anyway, this is what worked historically.

I am primarily a social and economic historian. In my work as a social scientist, I look at the history of equality and, yes, we don't have to choose between decommodification and redistribution because the two worked together historically and were incredibly successful together.

3 The moral limits of markets

Sandel:

Okay, let me press you on that. I see how they work together and can be mutually reinforcing, but it seems to me there are two reasons to be concerned about the excessive commodification of social and economic life. One of them is the one that you've been describing: that it makes money matter more and, against the background of economic inequality, it cuts people off from access to basic goods such as education and health and political voice. So that's clearly one important reason to worry about commodification and to want to decommodify social life. But I wonder what you think about a second possible reason to seek the decommodification of social life, which is not about equality or even about providing access to essential human goods. It's about whether putting everything up for sale cheapens or corrupts or degrades the meaning of goods, beyond obstructing access for those who can't afford them.

So, for example, we could take higher education. If education is highly commodified, then of course there is the question of unequal access, for which we've discussed a familiar objection. But doesn't it also lead students to view the purpose of education mainly in instrumental terms – getting a good career, making more money – and doesn't that crowd out or erode, in the attitude of students and ultimately of universities, a concern with the intrinsic good and value of teaching and learning?

Piketty:
Most definitely. And it also corrupts teachers. There are a lot of experiments showing that if you give financial incentives to teachers, linked to the grades their students get, you sometimes get higher grades to begin with, but then, when you ask students questions six months later about what they have really learned, you realize that they have not learned anything because the teachers have been teaching them to get good grades in the exam, not teaching them about the real stuff, the things that don't disappear six months later.

So, you are completely right, and I'm sorry if I didn't say that clearly, but in fact that's the reason, the key reason, why decommodification worked in the twentieth century in particular in the areas of education and health. We could take other examples in public infrastructure, in public transportation, in the energy sector, or culture – we could find many other examples in areas I think are going to become probably more than 50% of our economic system in the twenty-first century, if not 60 or 70 or even 80%. But if the decommodification process worked so well for education and health, it's precisely because this sort of intrinsic motivation that people have to work in education, to work in health, tends to be destroyed by monetary or profit motives.

Take the health system in the US. You put a lot of money into it for a long time. We used to say healthcare cost you 10% of GDP, 15% of GDP. Now it's 18%; it's going to be 20% soon. What do you get in terms of life expectancy, basic health statistics? Very, very bad outcomes. Why is it that some public systems in Europe are doing so much better with less money? Okay, maybe people are less well paid, the doctors in Europe are a bit less rich sometimes – they're already rich, but not quite as rich as in the US – but apparently they're doing a job that is at least as good.

I think by commodifying everything and giving higher financial incentives, higher pay, you destroy a lot of what people actually care about in their job, in their life. And this is not just a dream, this is based on the examination of how it works. Some people have tried to put a for-profit structure everywhere. You had Trump University, for instance, which was a for-profit university. This was a disaster. And even the most elitist schools and the most expensive schools to access – say Harvard University and Ivy League institutions – are not governed as shareholder companies. They're nonprofit institutions. That doesn't mean they're fair in their functioning. There are lots of problems with their admissions policy, with the way you get a seat on the board of Harvard, with lots of things, but at least you don't transmit mechanically your seat or your voting power to your children directly – or at least this should not be the way it works. And so there is less power for money in general, and for the private owner in particular. Would universities work better as shareholder companies? I don't think so because probably we would have destroyed what you at Harvard, or your students, cherish in an institution that is devoted to learning and research.

So, yes, decommodification is about intrinsic motivation, and this can be extended to other sectors including culture, transportation – and in the future, in my view, these are the sectors that are going to matter more and more.

Sandel:
Adam Smith suggested that tutors at Oxford should be paid according to the number of students who attend their lectures.

Piketty:
Maybe he was too much of an economist.

Sandel:
And Kant, in his first job I think, was paid according to the number of students who attended his lectures.

Piketty:
Yes, money had a huge role in education in the past. Today when we talk about legacy students in the US and the fact that the children of alumni or the children of donors can buy their admission, it makes me think about the end of Imperial China. We view Imperial China as a place that cherished examinations. And, indeed, you had very sophisticated entrance examinations to

become a higher civil servant. But you could also pay. So, there was a complex system where there was special access for the children of the Manchu warrior class, who were not particularly educated, but because of their warrior status wanted to be able to gain access for their children to some of the seats at the top of the civil service. But you also had some bourgeoisie who had a lot of money but whose children were not necessarily performing as well as they would like, and they managed to arrange the possibility of paying to compensate for this.

So, there's nothing new here. And I'm sure people were justifying this, not so much like Adam Smith or Kant talking about the motivation of teachers, but by explaining that, if you want to attract support for your institution, that's what you have to accept. Just like in the US today. So, yes, there's a rich history of such controversies. I'm not saying these arguments are always necessarily wrong or unconvincing. Some of these arguments we have to take seriously. But if we engage in some critical historical examination of these processes, I think the conclusion is that egalitarian decommodification has been a great success.

Sandel:

Now, here's the reason why I wanted to see if you agreed with this second argument for decommod-ification of social life, the one not to do directly with equality, but instead to do with corrupting the meaning of goods and social practices. The reason this seems to me more radical than, or at least more of a departure from, the mainstream social democratic project, and maybe at odds also with the way mainstream economists think about the economy, is that it requires us to debate and deliberate about the proper way of valuing goods. Economists – many mainstream economists – take for granted the de facto modes of valuation, the de facto preferences that consumers bring to economic life, and ask how to maximize their satisfaction subject to certain distributional con-siderations. But the corruption argument for decommodification, if we can call it that, would require that we debate the appropriate way of valuing health, education, cultural activities. And that would require us to put up for a political debate whether certain modes of valuation are higher, are worthier, than others. It would make economics and also public discourse more judg-mental than many social democrats, and certainly libertarians, would be comfortable with. Does a more judgmental mode of public discourse, and for that matter of economics, appeal to you, or is that something you would resist?

Piketty:
Oh, yes, that's appealing to me. Let me make clear that I don't identify myself that much as an economist. I view my work more as that of doing social and economic history – I mean somewhere at the intersection between socioeconomic history and political economy, in the old sense which recognizes the full moral and political dimension of political economy.

Let me also stress that valuation is already a political process. So, the idea that you can leave the issue of value to the market, to supply and demand, is not only unsatisfactory intellectually, but it's not actually the way it works. So even today – with all the limits of national accounts and GDP, and acknowledging we don't talk enough about inequality and that we don't take into account sufficiently planetary habitability in national accounts, to say the least – even with this very imperfect system, there's already a lot of political valuation in the sense that the value of health and education that are provided for free is determined by, in effect, the cost of production. So, technically, this means the wages and the input that we feel are necessary to produce education and health determine the value of education and health in national accounts. This doesn't come from a market process of supply and demand. This comes from a political deliberation process where we decide these things collectively through parliaments, through budgetary institutions, through political procedures which are certainly not perfect, but which are outside the market domain, and which in effect decide how much we're going to pay a public doctor in a public hospital, teachers in a public school. And that's going to be the value of education and health as recorded in national income GDP.

So, this political dimension of valuation is already there. Maybe today this component is 25 or 30% of the value production that's recorded in national income, that's counted this way. But in my view, in the future, it could be 50, 60, 70, 80%. So, yes, decommodification includes political valuation – what you call judgmental evaluation.

Going back to social democracy, is this a frozen product? Do we just need to continue a little bit further in what we have done? Or do we need something more radical? Again, I want to stress that historically social democracy was a radical project when the Labour Party came to power in 1945 in Britain, and even with Roosevelt in his own way, though it's a different political tradition in the US. It was the same with the Swedish Social Democrats and when the French socialists and communists came to power and put in place the social security system and public service in 1945. It was a radical project, and then it became mainstream because it was successful. We face the same challenge today. And for this, we need to address different major shortcomings to the twentieth-century social democratic tradition.

One is the fact that we've stopped the expansion of education and health. We need to continue this expansion. But then if you are really going to have a full generation going to higher education, you have to think about the quantity of resources you need to put into the education system – at some point, quantitative difference makes a qualitative difference – and you have to think about what it means to have an equitable admission process. You have to think about how to organize this very large social sector in general. The problem is that we have frozen everything to the level of the 1980s and 1990s. If you look at total public resources put into education, they were multiplied by 10 between 1910 and 1990, from less than 0.5% of national income in 1910 to about 5% or 6% of national income since 1990. But since then, both in the US and in Europe, they have basically frozen at this level, while the fraction of the generation going to higher education has increased enormously. We were at 20%, 30% of the generation at most in the 1980s. Now we have 50%, 60% – or even 70% in South Korea. If you make those increases with frozen resources, it means you are going to have some elite schools where people get a lot of resources, but a system where most people are going to public universities, or community colleges in the US, and don't get the resources.

So that's the first major limitation of the social democratic project we had in the past. The second one is lack of participation, not only in political deliberation and political life, but also in decision-making in corporations. A very important component of what I have in mind when I talk about participatory socialism is to have at least 50% of voting rights in corporations going to workers' representatives, even if they have no capital share. In addition, the other 50% going to shareholders should be strongly regulated, in the sense that a single shareholder should not have more, maybe, than 10% of the vote in large firms. So that, in effect, will democratize the decision-making process in companies in a way that is quite radical.

The third big limitation of social democracy in the twentieth century was the cross-national dimension. And that's really what I want to stress, which is that, historically, welfare states were built within the context of the nation states of the North, superbly forgetting about North–South inequalities and, even more importantly, the fact that the prosperity of the North would never have arisen without the existence of the South. In 1860, right before the US Civil War, two-thirds of the cotton used in the manufacturing of Britain or France came from the US South, from plantation slavery. And after slavery disappeared, it came from Egypt. It came from India. It didn't come from Britain or France. And this was similar for oil and fossil fuels in the twentieth century, for mineral extraction today.

So, it's a process of the global division of labor and the global exploitation of natural resources and labor that has made the North rich. And this is by far the most important limitation of the sort of social democratic and welfare-type capitalism that developed in the North in the twentieth century. And this is what has to change in the future. Otherwise, competition – and geopolitical competition from China in particular – will I think be an even more serious threat to the Western models than the Soviet threat in the twentieth century.

4 Globalization and populism

Sandel:
I want to pursue the question of globalization as it has played out since the 1980s. Now, you and I have both been critical of hyper-globalization and its insistence on the free flow of capital across borders, and on the free-trade agreements that were part of the neoliberal globalization project. People like us criticize the unfettered, unregulated

flow of capital and goods across borders, but we tend to be in favor of more generous immigration policies, which is the flow of people across borders. And those to the right of center tend to be critical of increased levels of immigration even as they endorse and promote the free flow of capital and goods. Which side is being inconsistent?

Piketty:
Well, actually, your question makes me think of my recent reading of the new edition of your book, *Democracy's Discontent*, which was first published in 1996. And I want to ask you about that book. So I'm going to reverse your question, which is one I really like. Just to summarize first what I understand in your writing. A new edition of *Democracy's Discontent* was published in 2022. And in this edition, in the introduction and most importantly in the epilogue, you make very clear, as you just said, how the excesses of globalization and the fact that left-of-center governments in effect supported free trade, globalization, financialization, and also the rise of meritocratic ideology – another topic I want to ask you about – contributed to the weakening of democracy and the fact that the Republican

Party broadly, and Donald Trump in particular, were able gradually to portray the Democrats as a party favoring the winners of the market.

Historically, the Democratic Party, like social democratic and labor parties in Europe, was a party supporting the working class, the lower middle class, and with very little support from the top of the income and wealth distribution. Now, this has been reversed, and I think, instead of blaming Trump and blaming the Republicans – which is always easy to do, of course – I think the Democrats in the US and comparable parties in Europe would be well advised to look at their own shortcomings. And something I really enjoyed in the new edition of *Democracy's Discontent* is the way you show that both the Clinton years, 1992 to 2000, and the Obama years, 2008 to 2016 – two very long, eight-year administrations with Democratic presidents – were also administrations that legitimated the neoliberal turning point of Reagan in the 1980s. I mean legitimated in the sense that the Democratic administrations continued – maybe this is something you emphasize less than I do – the demolition of progressive taxation started by Reagan in the eighties. Clinton and Obama did not really try to go against that.

And, more to the point, both administrations went very far into the direction of globalization and free trade, with the NAFTA agreement, the creation of the WTO, China's entry to the WTO just after the end of the Clinton presidency, and, under Obama, the Pacific Trade Agreement, which in 2016 at the end of the Obama presidency was opposed by both Sanders and Trump and never really applied.

Now, you are asking me, should we exercise more control over trade, capital, labor? I think you have to control something, and I think if you don't control free trade, you don't control capital flows, then indeed you'll see the nativist and nationalist alternatives promoted by Trump or Brexiters in the UK. They say, "Okay, let's control the labor flows." In the end, I think my answer is that we should control the capital flows and the trade flows much more. With the labor flow, of course, you need to have rules about how you pay for education for the people who come, how you pay for housing. All of this needs to be looked at very carefully. We are not just transporting commodities when people come with their family. You need to look at the social conditions of integration and you have to make sure that all the right conditions are met. But in the end, this is a challenge that can be addressed if we control capital flows and trade flows.

I think that's why we should be very careful to distinguish the different responses to the excesses of globalization. You have the sort of nationalist response – nativist, anti-migrant – which we see with Trump, which we see with Le Pen in my own country, etc. But then you also have what in the US was the Sanders response, which I like to call the democratic socialist response.

And one question I wanted to ask you about after reading your work – maybe one point of disagreement we might have – is how you use the term "populist" to describe these two different responses to the excesses of globalization. Of course, you make clear that this is not the same kind of populism, but still you use the term "populist," which, as far as I'm concerned, I would not use, because I think, well, there's a risk. The term can be, to me, part of rhetoric that's used a lot by people who claim to be in the center, but who tend to be mostly the winners of the market process and who like to delegitimate all their opponents by saying: "All my opponents from the left, from the right, are all populists."

So, using the same term to me is a bit risky, but maybe that's a French or European perspective, and maybe it's different in the US.

Sandel:
So, you would reserve it for right-wing populists?

Piketty:
I would not use it at all, actually. I would talk about "nationalist ideology," "socialist ideology," "liberal ideology." I think socialism, nationalism, liberalism are legitimate ideologies. They all have a point to bring to the democratic table, to the conversation. Calling them "populist" seems to me generally a strategy to delegitimate some of these groups. At least it can be used this way. I know this is not the way you want to use it, but so many people use it this way. And, as you were mentioning, restricting labor flows is very different from restricting capital flows. And so, if all opponents to free-market globalization are populists, then we're mixing up very different things.

Sandel:
Okay, well, let me try to address that. First, the use of "populism" – and this may reflect differences

in nuance or usage between Europe and the US, but the reason I use it to describe both Trump and Marine Le Pen on the one hand, and a figure like Bernie Sanders on the other, is that, at least in the American political tradition, the origin of the term "populist" in the nineteenth century was the coming together of industrial workers and farmers to try to win power from economic elites, typically northeastern economic elites who controlled railroads and later the oil companies. And it was a progressive movement, though, even then, it had nativist and antisemitic and racist elements. So these two strands – representing the people against the powerful, and this nativist strand – they've been present from the start. But in recent times, it seems to me that the success of right-wing populism, the authoritarian nativist strand, arises as a symptom of the failure of progressive or social democratic politics.

Piketty:
This, we agree on.

Sandel:
We saw this in the financial crisis of 2008, when first a Republican and then a Democratic

administration, in the transition from George W. Bush to Obama, bailed out Wall Street. In that moment of crisis, Obama had the choice of whether to restructure the relation of finance to the economy or to reinstate it, and he chose the second. I think this was a decisive moment for his presidency because it represented a departure from the civic idealism that he had inspired as a candidate in 2008, not only in the United States, but around the world – the hope and the expectation that this would be the beginning of a new kind of politics. And then when he took office just after the financial crisis, he appointed the same economists who had served in the Clinton administration, who had deregulated the financial industry. He invited them to try to fix things, and what they did was to bail out the banks and leave ordinary homeowners to fend for themselves. This prompted widespread anger across the political spectrum.

Now, Obama acknowledged that the bailout was unjust. He did not defend it in the name of justice. He said it pained him to bail out Wall Street, but he felt it was the only way, given the hold that Wall Street and big finance had on the economy. He wanted to save the economy. That was his rationale. But he did it, he said, with great regret.

The taxpayer bailout of Wall Street cast a shadow over his presidency. It dashed the high hopes for a revival of progressive or social democratic politics that his candidacy had inspired. And it generated two currents of protest: on the left, the Occupy movement, followed by the surprisingly successful candidacy of Bernie Sanders in 2016 against Hillary Clinton; on the right, the Tea Party movement, and ultimately the election of Donald Trump.

Both of these strands grew from the anger and outrage and sense of injustice at the bailout and the building back up of Wall Street, without holding anyone to account. So in a way, the progressive, mainstream center-left politicians who governed in the aftermath of Reagan and Thatcher laid the groundwork for the right-wing version of populism – of Trump in the case of the United States – that followed. They prepared the way for it and bear responsibility for it.

This takes me back to something that we were discussing earlier about the appeal of markets and of the neoliberal faith. When Ronald Reagan and Margaret Thatcher governed, they explicitly argued that government is the problem and free markets are the solution. They were succeeded by center-left politicians and political parties – Bill Clinton in the United States, Tony Blair in Britain, Gerhard Schröder in Germany – who softened the harsh edges of the laissez-faire capitalism of the Reagan–Thatcher years.

But they didn't challenge the fundamental premise, the market triumphalist premise – namely, that market mechanisms are the primary instruments for defining and achieving the public good. They never challenged that. And so, when they adopted neoliberal trade policies and the deregulation of finance during the 1990s and early 2000s, they were enacting that project and uncritically embracing the market faith. And so we never really had a public debate about where markets serve the public good and where they don't belong.

But here's a hunch. I want to go back to this question of judgmental, value-laden public discourse. On one level, mainstream politicians of the center-left and center-right were drawn to the market faith in part because of the belief that markets deliver rising prosperity and, at the

same time, yield Wall Street campaign contributions. But there's a deeper reason, I think, for
the appeal of markets and market mechanisms.
I think the deep appeal of the market faith during
this period, and perhaps for a longer stretch of
time, is that markets seem to offer a way of spar-
ing us as democratic citizens from engaging in
messy, contentious, controversial debates about
how to value goods and how to value the various
contributions that people make to the economy
and to the common good. So the market faith
arises – this is my hunch, but tell me whether you
agree or not – from a certain liberal aspiration
for neutrality toward substantive conceptions of
values and the good life. The idea is this: We
live in pluralist societies. We disagree about how
to value goods. We disagree about the nature
of the good life. So, ideally, we would like to
rely on instruments that are neutral, that spare us
from the need to make those decisions explicitly,
because we will disagree. Now, of course, markets are not truly value-neutral instruments. We
know that. But the misplaced hope that markets
can spare us from debating and deciding con-
tested questions about the common good is a
deep source of their appeal.

Piketty:
I agree with that. I think in the end, this is a fear of democracy. This is a fear of democratic deliberation.

Sandel:
Yes.

Piketty:
And this is a fear of what I refer to in my book, *Capital and Ideology,* as opening the Pandora's Box of redistribution, but also of the revaluation of what we do. The fear is we don't know where to stop and, okay, maybe we *don't* know where to stop. But in the end, our best chance to get somewhere is to accept this aspiration to self-government, which as you remind us in your writing is at the origin not only of some of the deepest aspirations of the US in the nineteenth century, but of modernity in general.

Let me come back just a little bit to this term "populist." I want to, because you very rightly said that Clinton, Obama, Blair, Schröder, were not able to question the new neoliberal Wall Street kind of ideology about globalization, financialization, meritocracy. I fully agree with that. They were not able to challenge this set of beliefs, but Bernie Sanders, and to some extent Elizabeth Warren, also in 2020, were able to challenge this by putting forward a platform that I like to call democratic socialism, because it goes even further than Roosevelt did in terms of progressive taxation. But it also involves a very substantial component of workers' decision-making power in corporations, with a strong representation of workers on the boards of companies. It also involves a very substantial decommodification strategy through public universities and a public health system. To me, this is not the expression of a sort of populist anger.

So, I'm still a bit puzzled why you want to label this "populist." I understand the history of the term in the US. As you said, with the early populists in the late nineteenth century and the early twentieth century, there was an uneasy mixture of progressive themes and nativist themes. I really don't see that in Bernie Sanders and Elizabeth Warren. So that's why I'm puzzled. Calling them "populist," I think, is giving too much weight to the way the Clintonians and the Blairists want to distance themselves from people further left.

Sandel:
I see. You worry that mainstream politicians use it as a term of abuse.

Piketty:
Yes, and in the end, the position looks very much more like democratic socialism to me, or social democracy for the twenty-first century, if you want. To me, that's a more precise way to describe what they stand for than "left-wing populist."

Sandel:
Here, maybe, is a nuance of difference in what it means. Populism is not mainly about redistribution, though it does for Bernie Sanders and Elizabeth Warren have egalitarian meaning. It's mainly about reclaiming power for the people from elites. And this is connected to economic inequality. But the populist strand, if it can be distinguished from the social democratic or democratic socialist strand, is less about redistribution than it is about reclaiming power, giving voice to the people, representing the people against the powerful, and reining in the power of big corporations in the economy.

Piketty:
But having more power for workers' representatives on the boards of corporations is exactly what reclaiming power is about. And both Elizabeth Warren and Bernie Sanders put on the table in the US Congress a very interesting proposal to extend voting rights for workers' representatives in very much the social democratic tradition.

Sandel:
We shouldn't worry too much about this, Thomas. There's an overlap. Clearly there is an overlap.

Piketty:
But it is the same term as the one used for Trump.

Sandel:
I see, so you don't want to use it.

5 Meritocracy

Piketty:
I'm still a bit concerned with your choice of terms. But, anyway, let me get to the issue of meritocracy

because I am a big fan of your book *The Tyranny of Merit*, which emphasizes the importance of this sort of religion or ideology of merit that has developed in recent decades. In your analysis, it's the third pillar of the neoliberal era. You have globalization, financialization, and meritocracy. I think you are giving it the importance it deserves. And so I wanted to ask you about this, and also, maybe most importantly, what are the ways out? At some point in your book, you advocate an Ivy League lottery that would work something like this. Assume you have, say, 100 places in Ivy League universities. You set a qualification threshold for admission so that you get 1,000 applicants with scores or grades above the threshold. Then you have a lottery to pick the 10% who are going to be admitted.

What I like here is that you don't want to let universities do whatever they want. If I understand you, this is part of the exercise of reclaiming control, an example of the democratic deliberation that should set rules about access to higher education or access to health. These are fundamental goods, and we cannot just let people on a board at Harvard decide what they want. Of course, some might say, "Well, after all, it's their university. They can do what they want. It's natural that they do what they want." To me, that's like when we say, "Okay, it's your money. You can send it to a tax haven and pay zero tax. After all, it's your money." Well, no, I'm sorry; this is not your money. This comes from the collective labor of millions of people. This could never have been produced without public infrastructure or our legal system. You are not on your own in the world, and you cannot just say: "It's my money."

Am I right to interpret what your specific proposal is on a lottery? There could of course be other proposals like this. It's just one example of taking back control in the sense that democratic deliberation should set these kinds of rules for admissions, including into Harvard and other top universities in the US.

Sandel:
Yes, it's partly that, and it's about something else too that goes back to this question about moral judgment, attitudes, and recognition. So, there are two problems with meritocracy. Before I identify the two problems, I should say, first of all, that merit in general is a good thing. If I need surgery, I want a well-qualified doctor to perform

it. That's merit. So how can merit become a kind of tyranny? Well, this goes back to the period we've been discussing, from the 1980s to the present. The divide between winners and losers has been deepening, poisoning our politics, setting us apart. This divide has partly to do with the widening inequalities of income and wealth that we've discussed. But it's not only that. It has also to do with the changing attitudes toward success that have accompanied the widening inequalities. Those who've landed on top have come to believe that their success is their own doing, the measure of their merit, and that they therefore deserve the bounty the market bestows upon them. And, by implication, that those left behind, those who struggle, must deserve their fate too. This way of thinking about success arises from a seemingly attractive ideal: the meritocratic principle that says, insofar as chances are equal, the winners deserve their winnings.

Now to the two problems with meritocracy. One obvious problem is that we don't live up to the meritocratic principles we profess. Chances are not truly equal. Children born to poor parents tend to remain poor as adults. Rates of upward mobility are limited. And take the example of the

Ivy League universities you've been asking me about. Yes, they offer generous financial aid policies. Students from families that make less than $85,000 a year – or $100,000 a year, I think, in the case of Stanford – pay nothing for tuition or room or board or books. Despite that, there are more students in these places from families in the top 1% than there are students from families in the entire bottom half of the country.

So clearly we are not a perfect meritocracy. But suppose we were. Suppose we could somehow create genuinely fair equality of opportunity for admissions in the educational system, and for that matter in the economy. Suppose we could do that. Then, with a perfect meritocracy, would we have a just society? I don't think so. That's because meritocracy, even a perfectly realized meritocracy, has a dark side: It's corrosive of the common good. And the reason it's corrosive of the common good is that it encourages the successful to view their success as their own doing, to inhale too deeply of their own success, to forget the luck and good fortune that helped them on their way, to forget their indebtedness, as you've been describing – their indebtedness to those who make their achievements possible.

Michael Young, who coined the term "meritocracy," was alive to this. He did not see meritocracy as an ideal but as a danger. And the danger was precisely this, that it would cultivate attitudes toward success among the winners and also among the losers that would drive us apart. It would cultivate hubris among the winners and humiliation among those left behind who were told, and perhaps persuaded, that their failure, their struggles, were their own fault. This sheds light on how our societies became so polarized in recent decades. As inequality deepened, as working people faced stagnant wages and job loss, mainstream politicians of the center-left and center-right offered working people some bracing advice: "If you want to compete and win in the global economy, go to university. What you earn will depend on what you learn. You can make it if you try."

What these elites missed was the insult implicit in their advice. The insult was this: "If you didn't get a degree, if you don't have a university diploma, and if you're struggling in the new economy, your failure must be your fault. You didn't do what we told you to do. The problem," they said, in effect, "is not with the economic policies we put in place. The problem is that you didn't improve yourself in the way we told you to." So it's no wonder that many working people without university degrees were angry. Their anger was directed especially against mainstream center-left parties that responded to inequality with what I call "the rhetoric of rising," exhorting those left behind to better themselves by getting a degree. This was the Democratic Party in the US, the Labour Party in Britain, the Socialist Party in France – parties now more identified with the values, interests, and outlook of the well-educated, credentialed, professional classes than with the working-class voters who once constituted their primary base. No wonder there was this backlash, this angry backlash. It reflects, I think, the way meritocratic ideas of success became the moral companion of neoliberal globalization.

Piketty:
Yes, I think you are perfectly right, or at least I fully agree with the diagnosis that what's so specific and so brutal with the contemporary ideology of inequality is this way of celebrating the winners and blaming the losers, which you don't

find in older inequality regimes. In past regimes, inequality could be very brutal, but you had the feeling that there was a sort of complementarity between the different social groups. Some people are nobles and warriors; some people are workers and peasants, and they're not necessarily stupid. We just need these different groups. I'm not trying to glorify those inequality regimes, but at least people were not trying to pretend that the poor deserve what they get and the rich deserve what they get. That is quite unique, I think, to today's inequality regime. It puts a lot of pressure on people and has concrete consequences on mental health and lots of pathologies. We see this is putting pressure on all sides of society – especially on poor groups, but also on children from upper groups who feel strong pressure to succeed. So I think you are right on target on this. But coming back to my question, because I'm always turning to solutions, I am wondering whether you would favor federal or maybe Massachusetts legislation to, say, ban legacy-student admissions and children-of-donor admissions and put in place some guidelines for admission policy for Harvard University and other Ivy League institutions.

Sandel:
Fair enough. To come directly to your question: I think Harvard and other private elite universities should get rid of legacy admissions.

Piketty:
But should we force them or should we just wait for them to do it?

Sandel:
I think that we should start by building public pressure and moral pressure to do it. And I think there's a good chance it will succeed, in part because the US Supreme Court struck down affirmative action for racial minorities. And that was always the implicit compromise. But now that it's not possible to take race or ethnicity into account, it's going to be very difficult for these universities to say: "But we can take into account whether your parents attended this place."

Piketty:
They do.

Sandel:
Well, they do, but some have begun to change. Johns Hopkins has rejected it.

Piketty:
Are they ready to give back the possibility of taking the children of rich donors?

Sandel:
Well, we'll have to see. I think we should work toward it. One way of taking a first step toward encouraging change through government action was proposed by Ted Kennedy, who, though a Harvard alumnus, proposed legislation to require these universities to make public the admissions rates for legacy children of alumni compared to applicants generally.

Piketty:
Transparency seems important, but when I look at this from afar, the other side of the ocean, I feel we should be a bit more radical. To me, we should require universities to have the same rules for admission for everybody, or possibly to give more chances to people with lower-income backgrounds rather than specific racial backgrounds, or at least to use more universal criteria than racial criteria, and not to give a special treatment to the children of rich donors. It seems a bit crazy that we get accustomed to the way

things are. I was mentioning late Imperial China, which had this kind of arrangement, but they got replaced by communist China after that. So I'm a bit concerned that in the US people have become accustomed to rules of the game which seem wrong.

Sandel:

I agree. We should get rid of it. And the question is how exactly. But certainly the universities should get rid of it and people should pressure the universities to stop doing that.

6 Lotteries:
Should they play a role in university admission and parliamentary selection?

Sandel:

I want to come to your question about the lottery. I first want to emphasize that what I'm proposing is a lottery among those who are well qualified. Places like Harvard and Stanford get some 60,000 applicants a year and they take fewer than 2,000. A large number of the applicants are perfectly well qualified to do the work and do it well, and to contribute to the education of their classmates. So, my proposal is to have the admissions committee determine who's qualified to flourish and benefit from the education in top universities. And from those qualified students – it may be only the best 25,000 or 30,000 of the 60,000 applicants – you would choose by lottery the 2,000 who are admitted.

The reason for this proposal is not mainly to achieve a greater mix of income classes. Now, that's important too. So important that I think perhaps there should be affirmative action, even though their test scores might not be quite the same as other students, to help those who would represent the first generation in their family to go to university or who come from low-income backgrounds. You could do that independent of the lottery, and I would be in favor of that. But the main reason for the lottery is to change the meaning of admission, and to change the attitudes toward winning and losing that the frenzied system of admissions now encourages. It would remind those who are admitted of what is true in any case under the current system: that there's a lot of luck involved. And to remind those who don't win admission of the same thing. It's a way of beginning to challenge or dampen the hubris of the winners, and the sense of defeat and demoralization of those who lose out.

Now this is in one small domain of social life, but you could consider uses in other domains, including in reforming representative or parliamentary government, especially in countries that have two houses. One could reform a bicameral legislature or parliament so one body would consist of elected representatives and the other body would be, not a House of Lords or, as in the US Senate, a system where small states are vastly disproportionately represented, but a house consisting of citizens chosen by lot. That goes back to an idea from Greek democracy. Or we could compare it to a jury. When we compose juries, it's by lottery. And if juries can decide matters of guilt and innocence, then why can they not deliberate about the common good along with a representative body?

This might be one way of diminishing the enormous role of money in political campaigns, and also of getting some rotation in office. It also goes against the credentialist prejudice that the age of meritocracy has created. The majority of citizens in democracies around the world do not have a university degree. In the United States, about 38% have four-year degrees. So nearly two-thirds do not. And in Britain, about 70% do not have a university degree. And yet what proportion of them are present in parliaments? Only a tiny, tiny number, only around 5 to 10%. The result is there are very few working-class members of parliaments in Western democracies. Is this truly representative? We accept it, and there's not a lot of debate about it. There would be debate if there were that vast a disproportion with regard to women in Congress or in the National Assembly or in the parliaments of other European democracies. We've made a lot of progress in bringing more women into representative government. So why do we accept so easily and without debate that people without university degrees have almost no presence in parliament? One way of breaking through that might be this idea where there are two bodies. We could have one elected, with suitable restrictions on campaign contributions, and have the other rotating by sortition.

Piketty:
I think this is very interesting, but in both cases I'm wondering if we can do even better than

lotteries. Let me take the two topics in turn, university admissions and then changing the social composition of parliament. If we think of university admissions, I want to contrast your proposal to choose by lottery from the pool of people with adequate qualifications with another proposal that you mention in your book, one made by Daniel Markovits, a Yale law professor, who would basically say the following to Ivy League institutions: "You do what you want, but at the end of the day I want you to have at least half of your students coming from the bottom two-thirds of the country in terms of parental income. You do what you want to redesign your admission system – lower the number of points necessary for admission for lower-income students, or whatever. But that's a minimum condition, and if you don't meet it then you will get sanctioned." He specifically mentioned removing their tax-exempt status. But I think you could do a lot more than that because you could insist that meeting the condition is part of their duties in regulating admission to a fundamental good, which is access to higher education.

My question about your lottery system, at least the way it is designed, is that, in terms of broadening social access to Harvard, it's not going to have an effect that will be quite as dramatic as what Daniel Markovits proposes. You mentioned earlier some statistics showing that right now we have more students at Harvard coming from the top 1% of the population than we have coming from the entire bottom 50%. I think this may be data for Harvard, Stanford, Yale. With your proposal, do you expect this to change? By how much as compared with a proposal like Markovits's where you don't necessarily need a lottery but that at the end of the day is potentially more ambitious?

Sandel:
Well, I think there are two goals here. One is the goal, which I very much favor, of changing the class composition of elite universities so that they enroll more students from low-income families. And that can be done either by conditioning the tax-exempt status on achieving a certain percentage of students from low-income families, or by urging universities to use affirmative action to admit more first-generation students and more students from low-income backgrounds. The goal of changing the class composition is important in

and of itself to provide more fair access. The lottery proposal might help a little with this, but by itself would probably not sufficiently increase the number of low-income students. That's why you need two different mechanisms. The lottery proposal has a somewhat separate purpose. It's directed at the second goal, which is to try to diminish the meritocratic hubris that's associated with admission, and even to lessen to some degree the intense pressure, the anxiety-inducing pressure put on young people throughout their adolescent years by families trying to prepare them to compete. It's partly to alleviate that pressure, to lessen the sense that where one ends up is all one's own doing. So a lottery and a Markovits-type plan have different purposes and I think we should consider both mechanisms.

Piketty:
So how would you combine the lottery with a Markovits-type plan?

Sandel:
Well, there are a few ways. You could set a certain percentage of the class you want to come from low-income backgrounds and admit them

directly, and then run the lottery. That would be one way. Or you could run the lottery and give extra tickets, so to speak, in the lottery to those from low-income backgrounds.

Piketty:
Regarding parliaments, I have the same question, which is that there are other mechanisms – maybe they could be used in conjunction with lotteries, or they could also be used as alternatives and might deliver equally ambitious or more ambitious outcomes. Let me take one example. Let's say we have 50% of the population right now that have no university degree, but only 5% of the members of Congress belong to this group. If you use a general lottery in the population for the second chamber, then 50% of the chamber will not have a university degree. So that's one way to improve what has sometimes been called "descriptive representation."

Now there's another way to do it. And here I'm reporting some proposals from someone I know well, Julia Cagé. Basically, she says you could require each party to have representative candidates running in constituencies. If the group you want to target is 50% of the population, then you need to have 50% of your candidates belonging to this group. And because you don't want the parties to put these candidates only in constituencies that are impossible to win, you make it clear the parties will get enormous financial penalties if at the end of the day they have less than 50% of their parliamentary group coming from this class of the population.

This is not just theoretical thinking by social scientists. You have a little country called India with a population of 1.2 billion and more voters than in the entire Western world, which since 1950 has been using a system where they draw at random 25% of the constituencies. And in this 25%, all parties need to present candidates from scheduled castes or scheduled tribes, which are historically the bottom 25% of Indian society. So, it's not exactly the mechanism I described, but it shows something like this has been done. The advantage of this kind of solution as compared to your lottery system is that you combine the advantage of descriptive representation with that of elections. You are not just going to draw at random any low-education or blue-collar worker. Everybody who might end up in parliament is going to have to be a candidate. They will have to show through political campaigns and collective deliberation what they stand for. Why would you prefer a lottery to this?

Sandel:
I think this is another interesting proposal and I'm sympathetic to it. It works better in systems where there are party lists.

Piketty:
No, it's a constituency system in India. It's the same electoral system as the US and Britain. The way it works is, okay, let's say you have 500 constituencies. You draw a random 25% of these constituencies and in these 100-plus constituencies, whether you are the Congress Party, the BJP party, or the Communist Party, you can choose the candidate you want, but this candidate has to belong to the scheduled caste or tribe. So, whoever wins will be a member of these groups. So, in parliament, by definition, you will have at least 25% of the targeted group.

Sandel:
It's interesting. I'm open to experimenting with various ways of doing it, and we'd have to study

the effects and the results, but I think that we should have a more robust public debate about how to improve the social, educational, and class composition of parliament. And I think all of these ideas are worth considering.

Piketty:
So you're not specifically just in favor of lotteries.

Sandel:
Right, and I'm not enough of an expert on how these ideas would work in various political systems, but I think we should put them on the political agenda.

Piketty:
Another issue which I think is important in this discussion about meritocracy is one which we have already mentioned: the issue of dignity. One thing that you stress repeatedly and convincingly in your work is the fact that the university system in the US, and throughout the world to some extent, has become a sort of gigantic sorting or ranking machine for young people. This is producing a lot of suffering. So, how do we exit such a system, apart from using this lottery system,

which is not going to solve this bigger part of the picture?

Sandel:
Right. For the bigger part of the picture, I think, first of all, we need to shift the terms of political discourse. We should focus less on how to arm people for meritocratic competition and focus more on how to affirm the dignity of work, how to make life better for those who contribute to the economy and to the common good – through the work they do, the families they raise, and the communities they serve – whether or not they have a university degree. There are a range of proposals that could be debated. Those on the left and those on the right may well disagree about what counts as the dignity of work and how to promote it. But that should be what we're debating, rather than focus on arming people for a competitive scramble up a ladder of success, while neglecting that the rungs on the ladder are growing farther and farther apart.

One of the most potent sources of the backlash against elites – we saw this in the Trump vote and we see it in votes for similar figures in Europe – is the sense among many working people and many without a university degree that elites look down on them, don't value the work they do. This has partly to do with the emphasis that we've been discussing in mainstream parties on addressing inequality mainly through individual upward mobility through higher education. So we should begin by recognizing that individual upward mobility through higher education is not an adequate answer to inequality. And we should also take seriously, those of us who are deeply critical of figures like Donald Trump or Marine Le Pen, the legitimate grievances of working people and people without a university degree against credentialed elites. This isn't always easy politically, partly because it's easier to blame figures like Trump and the racism and misogyny and the xenophobia that he does appeal to than to ask how the mainstream project of progressive politics in recent decades has contributed to the legitimate grievances of working people and those without a university education.

Here's one example. Isabel Sawhill, an economist at the Brookings Institution, did a study a few years ago on the amount that the federal government spends in the United States helping people go to university, in grants, loans, and tax credits. It amounted to $162 billion a year, whereas the amount the federal government spends in support of vocational and technical education is only $1.1 billion a year. $162 billion compared to just over $1 billion. Now, this reflects the credentialist, meritocratic prejudice of those who are making these policies. It's not only unfair, going back to the questions of distributive justice that we've been discussing, but it also conveys a lack of respect for the kind of work the working class does. And this is exacerbated, this lack of respect, this lack of recognition, by the outsized pay that goes to those in the financial industry. Why should a hedge fund manager make 5,000 times more than a teacher or a nurse, or for that matter a physician? It seems unfair and completely out of proportion to the value of the contribution of a nurse or a doctor or a teacher. That takes us back to the questions of value, valuing, and reevaluating social contributions. But it's also, beyond the unfairness, a kind of insult. It's a collective insult that our societies inflict, implicitly at least, on people who do work in the familiar sense of work, whether they be care workers or electricians or plumbers. Why do we not invest in their education and training to the extent we do for those who will be in the profes-sional classes? And why do we not value their work? In fact, a survey was done by some sociolo-gists about various prejudices against disfavored minorities. They gave people, first in Europe and then in the US, a list of commonly disfavored minorities. And the group that was most disfa-vored by respondents were the poorly educated.

So credentialism is in a way the last accept-able prejudice. Not that we've banished other forms of prejudice – far from it – but it's one that people almost unapologetically and unthink-ingly accept. So, the dignity of work, I think, is an important matter. It's important for the revival of social democratic politics because it's a way of recognizing that the problem is not just unfairness that can be solved by redistribution. It's also the lack of recognition, the lack of honor and esteem accorded to those without university degrees who nonetheless make valuable contribu-tions to the common good.

7 Taxation, solidarity, and community

Piketty:
I like this example of the complete lack of proportion in how much public attention goes to technical-training curricula compared with all the time spent honoring the small group who access the Ivy League. And I like what you say about the myth that if you put in sufficient effort, you will make it. And nobody talks about the vast majority of universities, public colleges, and technical-training schools which don't receive adequate resources. I want to stress that this kind of hypocrisy is very badly resented by a very large part of the population, not only in the US where you have a lot of inequality in access to higher education, but also in countries like my own country of France, which is supposed to have a publicly funded system in higher education, but where sometimes we put three times or four times more resources per student into the elitist schools than we put into a normal university or two-year colleges after high school. That's something that is not only unfair, but which indeed questions the dignity of the person.

I want to stress that the solution to this must involve a quantitative increase in the resources that we put into higher education. It's important at some point to be clear about the fact that if you want to address the rising need for health-care, hospitals, and higher education, it's simply not going to work if you try to do so with a sta-bilized share of national income. This is exactly, in the end, the contradiction in which we've been caught in recent decades. At some point we have to accept the view that the share of national income that we put into these public services and fundamental goods has to keep growing. Where is this going to stop? If you take European coun-tries, they had less than 10% of national income in tax revenue until World War I. They have 50% today. Is this is going to have to go to 60, 70, 80? I don't know. But it has to go up.

If you had told people 100 years ago in Europe that tax revenue would go to 50% of national rev-enue, well, people would have said, "Okay, this is communism, the sky is going to fall, the econ-omy is going to collapse, social order is going to disappear." Well, in fact, it happened, and it was a huge success historically. So, I think we should not be impressed by people today who know in advance that this number has to be frozen forever. In fact, it will not be frozen. If we don't improve services through public means, there will be more private resources put into health – just look at the US. There will be more private resources put into research, but at Google, Microsoft, or wherever, and there will be more resources put into education at private universities. It will all be very unequal. And in some cases, it will actually destroy some of the extrinsic motivation we were talking about earlier. So, from all viewpoints, it will not be good. The alternative is we have to accept the idea of increasing public resources, an idea that comes with committing to a more equitable tax system, a return to very sharply progressive taxation on both income and wealth. These are challenges that can be addressed, but on the condition that we realize the magnitude of the task.

This brings me to another question I wanted to ask you about, and to challenge you a little bit on. If we value dignity and want to return a more widespread sense of dignity to society, I think we have to compress the salary scale, the income scale, enormously. I'm not saying we should have complete one-to-one equality with all salaries, but I think one to five is sufficient. I could say a lot more about this, but that's my reading of the comparative historical evidence. Some people might say one to 10. But when the difference between the bottom and top is one to 50, one to 100, one to 200, then it's not just money. It's really a question of dignity because it means you can buy the time of other people, and this has very concrete consequences. You spend just a little bit of your income and you believe you can dictate what others are going to do with their time. And so the entire set of social relations is very badly influenced by these huge pay gaps. To me, you should have maximum wages – and minimum wages, of course – but we also need to return to very sharply progressive taxation. It's like taxing pollution. You want an 80%, 90% tax rate above a certain income level. That happened in the US for half a century. My reading of the historical evidence, and I've spent a lot of time on this, is that it actually worked very well.

Now, I'm wondering about the involvement of social scientists, but also philosophers, in this intellectual battle. And this is where I want to challenge you. I've always been puzzled when I read John Rawls's *Theory of Justice* from 1971, and I know you've been critical of Rawls. He writes in 1971, right at the time you have this long episode of very sharply progressive taxation in the US, though it was about to collapse. And on the right-wing side of thought at the same time, you had people like Hayek or Nozick or Milton Friedman who were very clear about what they wanted to do. They wanted to demolish progressive taxation entirely. They spoke about this all the time. And, of course, they were going to win the day in the 1980s.

Compare John Rawls to that. He is sort of in favor of progressive taxation, but he never takes a stand completely explicitly. You can read his entire book without any mention of the fact that there has been an 80–90% top tax rate in the US from the 1940s to the 1960s. So you can imagine that he's in favor, but he just forgets to say it. And I'm wondering whether this lack of appetite for a political fight about these concrete issues, in the end, was maybe not so good. The intellectual right was fighting to demolish progressive taxation, but the intellectual left was less eager to defend it. To me this partly explains why the conservatives won the battle.

When I read Michael Sandel today, 30 years, 40 years after John Rawls, I see a lot more appetite for getting into the fight about globalization. And in your new epilogue to *Democracy's Discontent*, what you say about the Clinton administration, the Obama administration, is rooted in history much more than is John Rawls's type of writing. But, still, you don't take a stand on progressive taxation or other concrete policy issues as much as I think I would like a philosopher to. So, I want to challenge you: If we want to have more dignity of labor, don't we need to compress very seriously the income scale, the salary scale? Don't we need to win this intellectual battle with the help of philosophers like you?

Sandel:
Okay, well that's a big challenge – to respond on behalf of philosophers in general, no less, as well as for myself. First on behalf of philosophers, a word in defense – a qualified word in defense – of John Rawls, whom, you're right, I criticize. I think it's possible to justify a more heavily progressive tax system with Rawls's idea of the difference principle, of helping the least advantaged members of society, and to

argue that his conception of justice requires that. It's possible to make a defense within his terms. So I want to defend him to that extent.

I think what was missing in Rawls, and it's my main criticism, was that he wanted to define and defend principles of justice in a way that did not depend on affirming any particular conception of the good or of the good life. My main argument was it's not possible, and it's not desirable, to detach questions of justice or of distribution from questions of the good life, of valuation, as we were discussing before. That was the main line of my disagreement.

Now, that's relevant to the contemporary debate about progressive taxation. And I'm very sympathetic to your arguments for more progressive taxation. However, I think that morally and politically the case for progressive taxation has to depend on being able to cultivate and appeal to a strong sense of community, a strong sense that, as fellow citizens, we are engaged in a common project with mutual responsibilities for one another and with mutual indebtedness. So I think the moral underpinnings for progressive taxation and redistribution can't be detached from these questions of identity, belonging, membership, community, solidarity.

Traditionally, socialist politics and philosophy drew heavily on notions of solidarity. Part of what Rawls was trying to achieve, maybe because he was writing out of the American experience, was to make the case for redistribution in a way that was compatible with a certain version of American individualism. And that's partly why – that, and also out of respect for a certain idea of pluralism – he did not want to base his case on any particular conception of shared identities, common purposes and ends. I think that was a mistake philosophically, but I also think it's a mistake politically for progressives and social democrats to try to make the case for progressive taxation without attending to the moral basis of commonality, of community, of identity.

So how do we create those conditions? How do we cultivate commonality? It can't be a purely abstract question. You make the point rightly, Thomas, that all wealth is a collective creation, not an individual achievement. This is important. But in order to feel and sense and believe that we are engaged in a common project, that we are mutually dependent and responsible for one another, we need to create within civil society conditions and institutions that remind us of our commonality.

So, here's a concrete proposal to further this idea of dignity and mutual recognition. One of the most corrosive effects of the widening inequalities of recent decades is that those who are affluent and those of modest means increasingly live separate lives. We send our children to different schools, as we've discussed, but we also live and work and shop and play in different places. The affluent secede from municipal centers and go to private health clubs. There are fewer and fewer class-mixing institutions in civil society, fewer and fewer occasions when rich and poor encounter one another in the ordinary course of their lives. We need to build a civic infrastructure for a shared life where people encounter one another, whether in health clinics or in public transportation or in public parks and recreation areas, municipal facilities, public libraries, sports stadia even. This inadvertent class mixing can create habits, attitudes, dispositions that remind us of our commonality. And so that's part of any project of creating a more equal society, even before we get to the tax rates, which I agree with you are essential. We have to create public places and common spaces that bring people together from different walks of life, that cultivate a sense of mutual responsibility and belonging.

I think, philosophically, that was missing from John Rawls's project. I think, politically, it's also been missing from progressive and social democratic politics over the past half-century, which is why I think any attempt to achieve a more equal society will depend on attending to the habits and attitudes and sense of a shared way of life that have been eroded by the growing gap between the rich and the rest. This is a practical observation, not strictly speaking a philosophical one – but it's connected to the philosophical idea that you can't detach the case for more progressive taxation, or for a more robust welfare state, from a certain shared conception of common purposes and ends. What do you think?

Piketty:
I fully agree with that, but I would say it goes both ways because you say you cannot defend progressive taxation and the compression of pay without emphasizing commonality, shared experience, civic values. I agree with that. But can you

stand for commonality without stressing progressive taxation?

Sandel:
No, they're reciprocally dependent. I agree. One depends on the other.

Piketty:
But when you say we have to wait . . .

Sandel:
Not wait. We have to work simultaneously.

Piketty:
So, I will wait for your next book then!

8 Borders, migration, and climate change

Sandel:
There's an even harder question, though, that this suggests. It has to do with the transnational dimension of equality and inequality, about which you've written. This is a special challenge if we agree on the dependence of a more equal society on stronger bonds among citizens.

If you are right that any project of equality has to have a transnational dimension, and I agree with you, do you think it will really be possible? What might that look like? Is it possible to create forms of allegiance and belonging beyond the nation state? We've had a hard enough time generating a robust sense of commonality even within the nation state. How can we build a federated, transnational form of redistribution and greater global justice while still attending to the importance of shared identities as a motivation for sharing resources?

Piketty:
I stand for democratic socialism, federal internationalist socialism. I would like some kind of United States of the World with progressive taxation. This will take a lot of time, though we are making progress with ideas like a minimal global tax on multinationals or billionaires. But, before that, I think we need to rebuild some new form of internationalism. First, as far as progressive taxation is concerned, there's a lot more that could be done simply at the level of existing nation states. If you take a country like the US, the federal government has ample state capacity to enforce

extremely progressive taxation without asking the permission of the United Nations or Europe or anyone. This can be done; this should be done; this could be done right away at the level of the US.

But if we take a broader look at transnational democracy, transnational justice, I think the big problem which you've identified very well is that center-left governments in recent decades have developed a religion of free trade, without any form of regulation, that has gone far too far. I mean that in the sense that, first, states gave people the right to move whatever they want between countries without any collective obligation. So, you could start by accumulating wealth in, say, the US, France, or Germany, by using all the public infrastructure, the legal system, schools, and hospitals, which your workers rely on, which you rely on. And then you acquire the right to press a button and transfer this wealth to another jurisdiction with no possibility for the national government to follow you, to tax you. And then the government tells the citizenry: "That's too bad. We don't know where the wealth has gone. There's nothing we can do." Except that it helped build this incredibly sophisticated international

BORDERS, MIGRATION, AND CLIMATE CHANGE

legal system which allows someone to press on a button and transfer the wealth away. There is a level of hypocrisy. We have started to build an international legal system that is made basically for the richest to completely escape their common duties, and then we pretend that this is natural.

That's the worst thing you can do to ideas of internationalism – a recipe to make people hate internationalism. It's very sad in a way that Donald Trump could pretend to be more moderate than this. Take the example of NAFTA, the North American Free Trade Agreement, which Bill Clinton pushed so much. In the end, it was Trump in the 2016 campaign against Hillary Clinton who looked more moderate about NAFTA, and in fact passed legislation that included the condition that if you want to export your automobile from Mexico to the US, you need to have a certain fraction of production that takes place on territories paying more than $20 an hour, or some similar wage condition. To be honest, the exact parameters were set in such a way that this legislation was not binding at all. It didn't have much of an impact on the level of pay in US production centers, so it was more gesticulation by Trump than anything real. But the very fact that it was a Republican administration under Trump that passed this kind of legislation to give a social and wage component to a NAFTA act passed by the Democrats shows you how things have turned completely upside down.

The same happened in my country when the Socialist Party was in favor of complete free-trade integration in Europe and the entry of China to the World Trade Organization. One of the best predictors of the vote for Le Pen in France even today is who voted "No" at the 2005 referendum on the European constitution, which was viewed as a sacralization of free trade and free capital flows. It's really these small cities, particularly in the northeast of France, which suffered a lot from job losses in manufacturing following the entry of China into the WTO, and which voted disproportionately "No" in 2005, that still vote a lot for Le Pen today. You have similar studies in the US showing that the localities and counties which had the biggest job losses due to Chinese competition voted the most for Trump. And according to some estimates, without these extra votes, Trump would not have won in 2016.

We have to take all of these facts seriously to realize that you cannot just blame the right-wing populists, blame their "deplorable" voters, their deplorable leaders, etc. I think the left parties and the center-left parties in power have to blame themselves and to realize that the way they built internationalism and globalization was guaranteed to make normal people hate it.

Because I am an internationalist and a socialist internationalist, I am particularly upset by this. So, how do we change this today? I think we have to start from the view that individual countries and individual governments have the right to set conditions for how they want to integrate in terms of economic relations and financial relations with the rest of the world. Let's take a very concrete example. Let's assume you're in France and that the country wants to tax corporate profits at 30%. There are other countries exporting to you – whether European countries like the Netherlands or Ireland, or other countries like China, Brazil, or the US – who tax corporate profits not at 30% but only 10% or 15% or 0%. You could assume a similar asymmetry with carbon taxes or other social or environmental rules. Then I think France should say, "Okay, you want to export goods and services to me, but from my viewpoint, there's a tax deficit because producers based on French territory are paying 30% corporate tax, but yours are paying 10%. So, there's a 20% tax deficit and I'm going to charge you the difference when you export your goods and services to me." This is not standard protectionism. The difference is that if the other country increases their tax rate to 30% or increases their carbon price to the same level as you, then the trade sanction will disappear. It's very different from standard protectionism in the sense that it's an attempt to try to bring everybody up to higher standards. Ideally, a fraction of the corresponding tax revenues should go to developing countries in the South so as to stress the universalist dimension of this policy. Now, if individual countries don't do something like this and just wait for unanimity or a very large coalition to solve the problem for them, nothing is going to happen.

I think at some point we need really to move off the standard map and accept solutions like this. You can say it shows a sovereign attitude, but I would call it "universalist sovereignism" in the sense that this is using universal criteria of social and environmental justice in order to define the conditions under which global economic integration can continue. Some people will be very unhappy. Some will certainly try to use the language of law to pretend that this is forbidden. They will use the law of the European Union. They will use of the law of the WTO. They will use legal language just as many conservatives have historically to pretend that, even if a majority wants to do something in a given country, they should not be allowed to do it. But at the end of the day, we'll have to do something like "universalist sovereignism" if we want to avoid the complete collapse of internationalism.

What's the alternative? The alternative, I think, if we don't do something like that to control capital flows and trade flows is to give the floor to the nativists who are going to control labor flows and to people who focus on identity. This will be ugly. It will not solve the social and environmental problems that we have to solve. Yes, some might say: "Okay, this will be a disaster, but at some point they will lose." Well, Trump lost in 2020 and came back to run again. I'm not sure we want to try that strategy for too long. There's a real risk that the so-called "progressives," or those who like to describe themselves as progressive, will in fact put themselves more and more in the situation of defending the winners of globalization. And when the reality they defend has become entrenched, it will be very difficult to change.

So, yes, internationalism has to be rebuilt, and this will have to come about by questioning the very foundations of the kind of free-trade and free-capital-flow regimes that were developed 30 or 40 years ago. I hope the change arrives in a peaceful manner through democratic mobilization. But it might also come through enormous pressure from the South because I think the big elephant in the room here is that the rise of unregulated free trade and Northern enrichment has come with the dramatic decline of planetary habitability, which is firstly targeting countries in the global South who are under pressure now to collaborate to fight in the Ukraine, and more generally to follow the agenda set by the North. But many countries in the South are thinking, "Well, look, you just think about your own profits, your own enrichment, but you don't care at all about all the damage you've done to us by being rich." So all this work to achieve a transformation of the global economic system, the financial system, the fiscal system, and environmental regulation is both to reconcile people in the North with globalization and internationalism, but also to reconcile the South and the North, so to speak, with some form of shared project. Otherwise, we will get to something extremely confrontational.

Sandel:
If I understand the proposal you've just now articulated, sovereign nation states, especially big ones, can enact unilateral policies to prevent companies from seeking out tax havens or moving capital and evading taxes within that country. But another approach, and maybe you consider this unrealistic, would be to try to get some global agreement or transnational institutions to set minimal corporate tax rates. Do you think that that's too difficult?

Piketty:
We have to pursue the two strategies at the same time. We need unilateral action of the kind I described in order to get the process moving. And at the same time, of course, we need to propose international cooperation. This could take the form of a minimum tax at the level of

the OECD or, ideally, the form of taxation on corporate profits and billionaires at the level of the UN. The process has started a little bit for taxation of corporate profits with most countries recently agreeing to a plan from the OECD for a minimum tax rate of 15%. But there are two main problems with this if you dig into the details. There are a lot of loopholes so that individual countries can escape the minimum tax rate of 15%. Plus, in any case, this minimum tax rate is too small and benefits only rich countries. Basically, poor countries in the South get less than 1% of the new tax revenue. So, really, it's a game between the tax administrations in Washington, Paris, and Berlin to split some of the tax revenues that are now in tax havens among them, leaving aside the countries in the South.

This I think is really unacceptable from the point of view of countries in the South who have asked for a long time to have a UN tax convention as opposed to an OECD tax convention – the difference being that the OECD is a rich countries' club. So, of course, the rich club members tend to split the revenue among themselves, whereas at the UN you have countries in sub-Saharan Africa, in South Asia, etc. Everybody voted at the UN General Assembly last year for a UN tax convention, except for Western Europe and the US. Of course, all the BRIC countries voted for this resolution, all of Africa, all of Latin America, and nobody speaks about that in the West. Everybody speaks about Ukraine instead, which is a very important issue in its own right, of course. But we ignore this issue of trust, national justice, and North–South redistribution.

This is wrong, especially after two centuries of development in the North, which again could not have happened without world resources in commodities, natural resources, and labor. There's the example of cotton that I gave earlier, and you have slave labor from Africa going to North America, producing the cotton that's used in European manufacturing as it pushes aside the Chinese and Indian production that was very strong in the early nineteenth century. We know all of this. It was written about a long time ago, but we tend to forget when we have concrete discussions about, for example, the OECD tax. So, yes, we need more international cooperation, but we need to do it in a way that is less hypocritical and really takes the South into consideration.

And we should not be too naive. I think in the end you need individual governments to do what they can right away, and they should not always use as an excuse the fact that they want a world coalition or unanimity, which of course we need to push for too. In Europe, I am in favor of what I call social federalism. I have pushed for a different form of European parliament based on national assemblies where, with majority rule, we could have a European-level carbon tax and a wealth tax. I would also push for a joint assembly between the European Union and the African Union, to have joint taxation to finance global public goods across the Mediterranean. So, I am a committed internationalist and federalist, but at the same time I think we need these unilateral strategies by countries to get us moving. We don't want to choose between the two strategies. We need both.

Sandel:
I wonder if we can discuss how this approach would apply to the debate about dealing with climate change. Now it's very difficult, as we've seen, to get countries to agree on their responsibility for reducing carbon emissions. And there

are hard negotiations that take place whenever we have global climate conventions. One device that some Western countries, and especially the United States, have pushed for in global agreements is to allow for tradable carbon emission credits. That means countries say they will accept more demanding commitments for reducing emissions if they are allowed to meet those targets not only by reducing their own emissions, but by paying some other country to reduce their emissions and to get credit for it. What do you think about that approach?

Piketty:
Well, this is an excuse for the US to not reduce their carbon emissions. I think not only is this not acceptable, but I think at some point in the coming years there's going to be a big backlash in the rest of the world. It's going to happen at some point. If you look at the accumulated carbon emissions of the US and Western Europe over the past 200 years as compared to the share of these two regions in world population, they have 60 or 70% of accumulated emissions for less than 20% of the population. If you add Russia and China, you get 80 or 90% of accumulated

emissions for less than 40% of total population. At some point, this has to create backlash.

There needs to be a huge reduction of emissions in the US and in Europe. Now, this has started a little bit, but from levels which are so incredibly high per capita. Sometimes people say, "Oh, but look at China," and it's true that the total emissions there now are very large, but you have more than 1 billion people in China. It's as if people in Switzerland were telling France, "Look, we have very small emissions." Well, they have a population that is 10 times smaller. So it's a stupid game. If countries with smaller populations pretend they can keep polluting because they have a smaller population, we are not going to get very far. We have to look at per capita emission level. And in terms of per capita emission level, the truth is that the US had more than 15 tons per capita for many decades. European countries had more than 10, 12 tons per capita until 1990–2000. It looks as if China is going to be able to develop without ever going above 8, 9 tons per capita. Of course, you can argue the technology has changed or that we didn't know as much 50 years ago. That's partially true, but at the end of the day, this is the way we have developed. This is the way we have become rich. We, you and me, we are not responsible for the choices these countries made 50 years ago or 200 years ago, but we are responsible for deciding not to take this into account in the way we look at our responsibilities today.

So what's the solution? I think one of the big battles we have between the nationalist ideology, the socialist ideology, and the liberal ideology, which I described earlier, is that nationalists like Trump or Le Pen are going to say more and more strongly: "Okay, you want to make us pay instead of China or instead of India. We don't want to pay." The problem is, if you want country-to-country redistribution – the US has to pay, France has to pay, and so on – then you will reach a dead end because nationalists are going to win the day because many people in the US, maybe even in France, in Europe, are going to say, "Well, look, I'm not so rich. Why should I pay? There are lots of very rich people in China. Why should I pay instead of them?" That's not going to work. So, this is why we have to move from a territorial representation of the conflict to something closer to a class conflict, where we want billionaires and large multinationals to pay whether they are in the US, in China, or in Europe. At the Paris Summit in 2015, rich countries committed to put money into climate compensation, but the amounts were far too small compared to the requirement for investment in green technology in Africa and South Asia. And even these very small amounts have not been disbursed yet. I think, as long as we require governments to make these payments out of their general budgets, this is not going to work.

Instead, we need a targeted, specified fraction of a global tax rate on top billionaires, on multinationals, which goes directly to countries in the South in proportion to their population, and maybe in proportion to their exposure to climate change. We were referring earlier to a minimum tax rate on multinationals or billionaires. I think a fraction of this should go directly to each country in the world, independently of whether there's a tax base, whether billionaires or multinationals have specifically invested in the country or not. Because if you take a broader look at climate damage and 200 years of industrial development on the planet, the point is that all countries are exposed to climate change, especially in the South.

You have to go back to a basic view about the right to development, the right to self-government, the right to self-determination. And this requires minimum tax revenue for sub-Saharan Africa and in South Asia, to invest in green energy, solar energy, to invest in schools and hospitals. The only way to make this acceptable to public opinion in the US or France is to target specifically high-wealth, large corporations that will pay directly. Short of that, this is not going to work. And if we don't do anything like this, again, the geopolitical competition is going to come from China and Russia, who are going to propose some other funding mechanism with requirements in terms of political influence that are highly questionable. But if Western countries don't propose something more acceptable, this is what's going to happen. It is quite clear.

Sandel:
Let me test your international socialist principles with a question about borders. Is there any good principled reason not to have open borders?

Piketty:
I think it's the same question. You have different levels of government – in your neighborhood, your

region, the country, your continent, the world. We have to look at each of these levels. What are the "costs" and benefits of self-government versus international cooperation?

To be more specific, I think the free circulation of people always comes with some specific public goods that need to be financed, whether it is education, transportation, or the environment. To take an example, European Union member states have decided that you are free as a student to go to any EU country where you want to study. I think it's a fantastic principle, one of the great achievements of the European Union. The only problem is that we didn't plan anything to pay for this university funding. You could be in a situation where the French taxpayers or the German taxpayers pay for the student to go to university, but then the student moves to another country, and there's no common federal income tax in Europe. It's a very strange system because, in the end, the system is underfunded. So we should plan common funding. Now, what we do with the rest of the world raises similar issues. What we've set up in the past 10 years in Europe is to charge very high tuition fees for students from outside Europe.

Right now, the situation is, if you take a student from Norway or Germany in French universities, they pay close to zero. But if you take students from Mali or Bangladesh, they have to pay 5,000 euros or 10,000 euros each to come. Is this the best we can do? I'm not sure. I would like us to have more free circulation, greater possibilities for students to come. But this would have to come with some international tax regime that will pay for it.

That's a specific example or answer to a general question but it illustrates the general point I want to make. If we plan sufficiently well the funding of public services, whether these are universities, hospitals, housing, transportation, or infrastructure, I don't see any reason to have strong restrictions on free circulation. Of course, that's a big if. But the point is that, in my view of democratic, federalist, and internationalist socialism, we should be very close to free circulation and open borders.

Sandel:
So, at the moment, do rich countries have a right to keep out migrants from poor countries who want to come?

Piketty:
What do you mean by a right? I think we all have a right to think of a better system. We all have a duty to think of a better set of institutions. And so, if you're asking me, is Europe right now sufficiently open to the rest of the world in migrant flows, my answer is no. Our current strategy is to say we need to have 10,000 more or 50,000 more people die in the Mediterranean to ensure that nobody else wants to cross. Is this the best we can do? Are we saying "We've thought a lot about it. And after 2,000 years of civilization around the Mediterranean Basin, this is the best solution we have found to regulate human flows." If you're asking me if this the best solution, then, no, this is not the best solution.

We've never been as rich as we are today. So, of course, we could do much better than that. But I think this is yet another example where, because we've given up on some ambitious continuation of the egalitarian agenda of making the most powerful economic actors accountable to democratic control, making them contribute to the public goods we need to fund, you have this nativist discourse of blaming migrants or supposedly excessively open frontiers for our problems.

In fact, the magnitude of the flow as compared to the European population of 500 million is relatively small.

9 The future of the left: economics and identity

Sandel:
The reason I'm pressing you on this, Thomas, takes us to something we should discuss before we finish: the future of the left. It seems to me that one of the greatest political vulnerabilities of social democratic parties is that they have allowed the right to monopolize some of the most potent political sentiments, namely patriotism, community, and belonging. Immigration is an issue that forces us to ask questions about the moral significance of national borders and, by implication, about the moral significance of nations as communities of mutual dependence and responsibility.

My sense is that the future of a left politics will depend on developing fuller answers to these kinds of questions. I think it's a mistake to cede patriotism to parties of the right. It seems to me that social democratic and progressive parties should articulate their own conception of what patriotism and belonging mean. For example, when companies seek tax havens rather than pay taxes in the countries where they sell their goods and make their profits, couldn't this be described as a failure of economic patriotism? Don't companies have a patriotic duty to pay taxes and contribute to the common good in the country that makes their success possible?

But, beyond this example, do you agree that parties of the left have had a hard time, especially in recent decades, articulating an ethic of membership, belonging, community, and shared identity? What has become of the left's traditional emphasis on solidarity, civic pride, and the mutual obligation of citizens? A healthy sense of civic pride can offer an alternative to xenophobia and hyper-nationalism. And isn't it also necessary to support the more generous welfare state that social democrats and democratic socialists care about?

Piketty:
First, I think what explains the vote for Trump or the vote for Le Pen is primarily, if you really look

at the specific places where they are getting a lot of votes, job losses – in particular, job losses in manufacturing due to trade competition – rather than an inflow of migrants. And I think it's very important to see that. So if you try to explain the places where you have a very high Trump vote or very high Le Pen vote by using the inflow of migrants or the proportion of people with foreign origins or extra-European origins in the population, you explain very little.

Sandel:
But the salience of the immigration issue is high in some places with very few immigrants. Why is that?

Piketty:
It's not as if there was no observable event that explains things. There's another observable event which explains a lot, which is the destruction of jobs. Let's address this. You are asking me why the left has not been able to respond. Well, because they have not addressed the issues of trade and jobs. They will not win by competing with the nationalist right on identity discourse or about migrants because the nationalist right will

always be more convincing on this front. What's important, I think, is to address what's really the core issue for the voters. In the US, it's very clear that in the counties where Trump has been getting the most votes, the big predictor is job destruction in manufacturing. It is not the inflow of migrants from Muslim countries or wherever. This is just wrong.

We see the same evolution in France. It's very clear that the voters who historically voted for the National Front, for Jean-Marie Le Pen, the father of Marine Le Pen, were more in urban areas and lived close to a migrant population. And there were historically among Le Pen voters people who were clearly angry at North African migrants. These voters were completely absorbed first by Sarkozy, by the free-market right-wing party LR, and many also voted for Zemmour in 2022, a very, very strongly anti-Muslim candidate, much more violently anti-Muslim in a way than Le Pen, but very free-market on economic issues. Now Zemmour is getting a very bourgeois racist vote, if you want to call it that, and a very urban vote. What is left to the Rassemblement National, which is the new name of the National Front, the party of Marine Le Pen, is a vote that

THE FUTURE OF THE LEFT

you find in small cities with no migrant population and where the real issue was opposition to European trade integration and opposition to the European Treaty of 2005.

Sarkozy, when he was in power in France, was the voice of the liberal right and the free market. He tried to appeal to these people by being very strong on identity. He did that very strongly. He said, "We have all these young boys and girls, especially young boys, coming from North Africa. We need to get rid of them. We're going to send policemen everywhere." But at the same time, he wanted to ratify the European Constitutional Treaty of 2005 through parliament without changing a comma, a treaty to which the people had already said "no" in a referendum. Now these voters said, "Okay, you think you're going to get us just by being violent to North Africans, but basically, we don't care about that. Our main problem is trade competition. Whether it's from Turkey, from China, from Algeria, from Mexico is not the issue. The issue is that we are losing jobs."

Another issue, and I think it's very important for the US too, is that people in small cities are always being stigmatized. They're criticized, for instance, for having their own car, for having individual houses. And they're told by people in the capital cities that they are responsible for climate change, for carbon emissions. Then people in the capital cities will take a plane to Rome for a weekend; they have emissions which are much, much bigger. I think these issues of job loss, trade, competition, transportation, housing, are the concrete issues that have led to this feeling of being abandoned by both the center-right and the center-left, much more than issues of identity. You can see that the politicians who have tried to compete with the nationalist right on identity – Sarkozy and Zemmour in the French context – were not able to attract these voters, who are really asking for change in how economic globalization and the economic system are organized.

To summarize, I think the problem of the left is not only that they have not questioned the way the economy has been organized, but that they have been the champion of its evolution, as you yourself have very well shown. This is a challenge that has not been seriously addressed because the left today basically says, "Okay, we should get some international agreements, we should get some international agreements, we should get some international agreements." And then if they don't get them, what do they do? They do nothing at all. That's why this sort of unilateral action I was describing earlier is very important. As long as the left say, "Okay, we are waiting for some international agreement on common taxation and carbon taxation and everything," it's basically telling the public "There's nothing we can do without others agreeing. Except for one thing. There's only one economic policy we can follow, which is to control our borders with respect to migrants and identity." Now, if you tell that to the public over many decades, if you pretend that's the only thing you can control, you should not be surprised when the entire political discussion is about border control and identity. I think that's a trap, something that should be avoided at all costs because, in the end, this will lead to victory for the nationalist side.

Now, the nationalist side also has a point. Again, if you look at political conversation since the Industrial Revolution, it has involved, to simplify, three big ideological families: nationalism, liberalism, socialism. I think each of these main families has a point. Liberalism has contributed through its insistence on a plurality of views and political issues and in its emphasis on market forces. Competition has contributed to prosperity to some extent, except that it came with enormous social costs, social damage, environmental destruction. And then you have two main responses to the challenges coming from liberalism. You have nationalism, which stresses ethno-national solidarity. It's not necessarily completely stupid. It can work in some cases. You cannot just have a world government right away. You need to have more local interests and solidarity at the level of local community. But there are also many limits on the kinds of problems this ideology can solve, and it has often been used as a veil to preserve the power of traditional local elites. And then you have various forms of internationalist socialism or democratic socialism that are trying to build a different and alternative economic system. That's very difficult, but it has been incredibly successful, with the rise of social democracy, decommodification, and progressive taxation. I don't pretend we need only one pillar for democracy to work. We need each of these three pillars to be strong. But the socialist pillar or the left-wing redistributive pillar has been weak since the fall of the Soviet Union. We need it to be strong again if we want democracy to function at the national and transnational levels.

Sandel:
I think there may be a nuance of difference here. Let me see if I can try to describe it and you'll tell me if you recognize it. I think I would distinguish less sharply, Thomas, than you do between identity issues and economic issues. Of course, I agree that the job losses due to the trade policies of the age of hyper-globalization have had an enormous political impact in driving up support for figures like Trump and Marine Le Pen, and likewise the dislocating effects of unfettered capital flows and the financialization of the economy. But there are two kinds of effects here. One is the direct economic effect: job loss, wage stagnation. The other is an effect that is connected to a politics of identity construed more broadly than border policies or immigration – identity in the sense of speaking to the expressive dimensions of politics. We talked about dignity and recognition. And it seems to me that people who lived in hollowed-out industrial towns suffered not only wage stagnation or job loss. They also suffered

the sense that the rest of the society, or those who governed it, didn't care about them as fellow citizens, didn't recognize them or respect them or care about their dignity.

Piketty:
Even stigmatized them for being responsible for climate change.

Sandel:
Yes. Your language of stigma draws on the language of recognition, identity.

Piketty:
Definitely. At the end of the day, it becomes a matter of identity. I agree with that.

Sandel:
Okay, so I want to connect this idea of stigma, of elites looking down, to the politics of identity, in the sense that it's part of the politics of recognition and belonging. As I see the future of the left, while we're discussing it retrospectively as a diagnosis, but also prospectively as what would be required to create the conditions for social democratic politics, it seems to me that

we can't ignore the politics of recognition. That is a kind of politics of identity, though not the same one . . .

Piketty:
No, it's not the same one.

Sandel:
But we need to articulate it and, in articulating it, we have to recognize and name grievances.

Piketty:
But it's not the same one.

Sandel:
But it's still within that territory. It's not a purely economic thing like job loss.

Piketty:
There's no purely economic thing. It's always multidimensional. It's a set of aspirations that we are talking about. We referred to being stigmatized for having your own car. So, yes, ultimately it becomes identity, but it's a very different form of identity than the one stressing ethnic origins and religion or the color of skin.

Sandel:
Fair enough.

Piketty:
Yes, and the left does have to speak to that kind of identity, and to respond to it. I think the criticism made by Trump and Le Pen, which works politically – maybe particularly in the US – is anti-elitism. Back in the 1980s or 1970s or 1960s, the economic elite, the educational elite, all the elite voted Republican. The Democratic Party had a very low score with elites. It's different if I look at data now, and I'm using for the US the same kind of data we used in our recent book on French elections. At the local level, if you look at the fanciest areas, the most affluent places, they would historically have voted Republican. This has changed. And this started much before Trump, and this is what made Trump possible in a way. Now the richest places actually vote Democrat, and this is what has made possible the Trump Republicans. But it could have been someone else who said: "Look, these people pretend to be in favor of equality, but they're all liars. In fact, they just defend their own privilege." You can see where they are. Yes, they're at

Harvard, but they're also in the fanciest areas of the country.

I want the Democrats to lose their vote in the wealthiest areas. As long as they have a big majority of the vote in these areas, it means that there's something wrong in what they propose, and they won't get the vote in poor areas. It means that they will always be portrayed by the other side as being elitist. But the way to appeal to non-elites is not to have a race with the Republicans on identity in the sense of concern about migrants.

Sandel:
Not in that sense, no. What you say reminds me of an experience I had this winter. My family and I were vacationing in Florida, and I got into an elevator in the place where we were staying. An older woman who was in the elevator asked me, "Where are you from?" And I said, "Boston." That's all I said. She replied, "I'm from Iowa." (That's a state in the center of the country, in a Midwestern farming region.) And then she added, "And we know how to read in Iowa." I didn't know what to reply. I hadn't said I was from Harvard. All I said was Boston. Then, as she got out of the elevator, she said, "We don't

much like people on the coasts." This, in a way, is a politics of identity. It's not about immigration, but it's about feeling looked down upon. It's about recognition. It's about dignity.

Throughout this conversation, we've discussed three aspects of equality. One is economic, about the distribution of income and wealth. A second is political, about voice and power and participation. Then there is this third category, about "dignity," "status," "respect," "recognition", "honor," and "esteem." My hunch is that this third dimension is the most potent politically, and maybe also morally. And that any hope we may have of reducing inequality in the first two dimensions, economically and politically, will depend on creating the conditions for greater equality of recognition, honor, dignity, and respect. It's a hunch. I can't prove it. What do you think?

Piketty:
This seems very reasonable to me. And to return to one of the themes we alluded to, I think the sort of democratic socialist agenda promoted by Bernie Sanders and Elizabeth Warren, and hopefully by younger candidates and maybe less-white

candidates in the future, will continue in this direction. I think pushing in this direction is one of the reasons for the success of this agenda, especially among the young voters – and when I say young, I refer to the fact that, among people below 50, Bernie and Elizabeth Warren were far ahead of Biden. I think it's by continuing in this direction that the Democratic Party will be able to restore hope and a feeling of recognition to a larger part of the country than just Boston and San Francisco. Similar conclusions also apply in Europe and elsewhere.

Sandel:

To conclude our conversation, I brought a passage from Jean-Jacques Rousseau's essay on the origins of inequality.[1] It fits with a theme that's run through our conversation, Thomas, because he first seems to locate the origins of inequality in the invention of property. But then he explains that even that invention was only possible because of a change in attitudes having to do with the way we recognize and look upon one another. So I'd

[1] Jean Jacques Rousseau, "Discourse on the Origin and the Foundations of Inequality among Men" (1754).

like to read you this passage and see whether you would interpret it that way.

First, the property account of the origin of inequality: "The first man, who, after enclosing a piece of ground, took it into his head to say, 'This is mine,' and found people simple enough to believe him, was the true founder of civil society." And then Rousseau goes on to say: "How many crimes, how many wars, how many murders, how many misfortunes and horrors," could have been spared if someone had "pulled up the stakes . . . [and] cried to his fellows, 'Don't listen to this imposter. You are lost if you forget that the fruits of the earth belong equally to us all and the earth itself to nobody.'"

That in itself is pretty powerful. But then Rousseau adds this: "This idea of property depends on several prior ideas," a "slow succession of events and mental improvements." (Rousseau is speaking ironically when he calls them "mental improvements," because, remember, for him, civilization brings a kind of corruption.) He imagines a primitive state of humanity when people were not self-conscious and didn't compare themselves. And then, over time, they began to assemble around a great tree, singing and dancing: "Everyone begins to survey the rest and wishes to be surveyed [or looked upon] himself. And public esteem acquires a value. He who sings or dances best, the handsomest, the strongest, the most dexterous, the most eloquent, comes to be the most respected." This competition for honor and recognition, Rousseau says, "was the first step toward inequality." Do you think he was right?

Piketty:
We would need to spend more time talking about Rousseau's text, but I think both parts of his statement are important. I think the second part can also be related to what you say about merit. I think the origins of inequality and the origins of the problems we need to address are multiple and come both from inequality in property and from inequality in talent, which people will then try to give moral meaning to so they can justify the winner and stigmatize the loser. All of this is important, and indeed all of this is in the text of Rousseau.

But one thing on which Rousseau, I think, is very clear, is that the problem is not so much the initial enclosure and the initial piece of private property, but rather the accumulation of property without limit. This is very clear in Rousseau, and that's also the view that I'm trying to develop. The problem is not the people who own a house or who own a car. The problem is the incredible concentration of property in a few hands, and this comes with concentration of power. Some people have a lot of power, some people have no control.

So, wealth and property ownership are about more than just money. They are about bargaining power that you have vis-à-vis your own life and vis-à-vis the rest of society. When you don't own anything or when you only have debt – another thing Bernie tried to address by suppressing student debt – you need to accept every working condition, every wage, because you need to pay for your rent. If you have a family, you need to pay. If you own just $100,000, $200,000, $300,000 – well, from the point of view of a billionaire, that's like zero. There's no difference between this and zero. But in fact, it's very different because you can make plans. You can buy a home, maybe not in New York or Paris, but in lots of places in the country you can buy a home. You can start a little business. You can start being a little bit more picky about the jobs you are being offered, which is what employers and property owners don't like. But maybe your being picky is something we want to have. So it's really more about power, bargaining power. Where I agree with Rousseau is that the problem is accumulation, the boundless accumulation of private property itself.

Sandel:
Well, we've covered a vast terrain in trying to explore what equality means and why it matters, ranging from income and wealth to power and voice to dignity and recognition. Like Rousseau, we've found that thinking about the meaning of equality prompts us to traverse economics, philosophy, and political theory. I hope this is a conversation that will continue. Thank you, Thomas.

Piketty:
Thank you, Michael.